Legends, Myth of Wessex

GW00697174

Roger Crisp

Contents

WESSEX BOOKS
A Member of the Independent Publishers Guild

Ghosts

What better way to introduce the subject of ghostly stories from Wessex than through this eerie extract from Hardy's poem *The Glimpse*.

She sped through the door
And, following in haste,
And stirred to the core,
I entered hot-faced;
But I could not find her,
No sign was behind her.
'Where is she?' I said:
– 'Who?' they asked that sat there;
'Not a soul's come in sight.'
– 'A maid with red hair.'
– 'Ah.' They paled. 'She is dead.
People see her at night,
But you are the first
On whom she has burst
In the keen common light.'

THOMAS HARDY, *c.*1900

Sandford Orcas Manor, near Sherborne, Dorset

This manor house can claim to be one of the most haunted buildings in the country. The documented unearthly visitors include: a grey lady thought to be the grandmother of an eighteenth-century occupant; a man in modern dress; a man in a shepherd's smock; music from a harpsichord or spinet; voices in several parts of the house; furniture and a picture that move; a window that opens itself; knockings on doors; curtains that open and close without aid; ringing bells; footsteps on staircases; yearly visits from a Moorish servant who was strangled with cheesewire; a group of cowled monks; murders that re-enact themselves; a naval cadet buried in the wall behind a bedroom; an Elizabethan man and woman; and more recently, two previous occupants, Colonel and Mrs Claridge. A great deal of scepticism accompanies this panoply of spirits, yet there have been many people over the decades willing to testify to the truth of their experiences.

Ghosts are rarely thought of as modern but this story involves a car crash on a bridge in August 1965 when three people in a mini crashed with a lorry and were killed. Two years later a young man on a motorbike was passing over the bridge, when three people suddenly walked out in front of him. As there was no chance of avoiding them, he drove his vehicle straight through the group. Strangely, on looking back, he saw that he was alone on the bridge. His victims had vanished into thin air.

Sturminster Newton, Dorset

In St Margaret's churchyard lies the grave of Florence Nightingale. Her ghost has often been seen inside the church where she has attended many services.

East Wellow, near Southampton, Hampshire

In 1952, whilst on holiday in the New Forest, a family from Somerset came across a large lake. In the centre of the lake, about 50 yards from the shore, stood a large boulder with a sword embedded in it. The family presumed it was a memorial to King Arthur and vowed to return the following year. Strangely, they were unable to locate the lake a second time and over the years have made more than two hundred trips to try and find it again. They have not yet been successful, so it seems that what they saw was a ghostly apparition.

New Forest, Hampshire

In the 1950s a photograph was taken of thirteen phantoms standing in front of the altar at Winchester Cathedral. One of these figures, a limping monk, haunts Cathedral Close to this day.

Winchester, Hampshire

Cudworth, near Crewkerne, Somerset	The local vicarage is haunted by a ghost that falls downstairs. The deceased was apparently pushed down by a brother or son, and died as a direct result. A recent rector heard the tumbling noise and thought that his mother had had a bad fall. Oddly, the noise seemed to come from a place where there were no stairs and eventually he discovered that a staircase at the spot had been removed by a previous owner.
Holford, near Watchet, Somerset	Fox hunting has become a very contentious issue and the ghost of a bloody and ragged kennel-man, who walks the Holford hills, could explain why. The local Dog Pound is thought to have been built to round up stray dogs for collection by their owners. Before cold storage was possible, foxhounds would be kept in kennels with their meat hung from nearby trees, well above the reach of congregating strays. If anything went for their meat the hounds would make a great din. On one such night, at this particular stone-walled pound, the kennel-man got out of bed in the early hours, not caring what clothes he put on, and went with his whip to put an end to the racket from the foxhounds. It is presumed that, not smelling his normal kennel-man's jacket and clothes, the hounds did not recognise him and tore him apart in a great frenzy.
**Taunton, Somerset**	Judge Jeffreys left his bloodthirsty and uncompromising imprint on the history of Somerset and the rest of Wessex, when he was sent from London to judge the 'guilty' followers of the rebellious Duke of Monmouth. The 'Bloody Assizes', held after the Pitchfork Rebellion of 1685, was quick to hand out the death penalty. Often the executed were cut up and their limbs boiled in tar before being distributed for display on crossroads and village squares, as a grim warning not to think of rebellion again. Jeffreys was thorough then and is persistent even now, as his ghost wanders Taunton's castle grounds, usually in September.
Langley Burrell, near Chippenham, Wiltshire	Ghosts, or at least the stories concerning them, can become confused. Reginald de Cobham was the young lord of the manor in 1413 and a supporter of the then heretical John Wycliffe. The young man was taken to the top of nearby Steinbrook Hill and condemned to death by slow roasting over a fire. His naked ghost roams the hill, carrying his head under one arm.

Ghosts have usually had enough of dying, so the apparition of M Dormitory in B House at the local College is unusual. One former pupil wrote in 1888 that the 'gentleman occupies his time throwing himself out of the window, apparently to remind spectators of the crowning folly of an ill-spent life'.

Marlborough, Wiltshire

Some seventy-five years ago a man who lived in the small village of Newton Toney claimed that he had encountered some very strange goings-on in the grounds of Wilbury House. He quite often passed through the estate on his way to work and to cross the drive it was necessary for him to pass through two gates known as the 'Double Shutte'. On his return from work one evening, as he made to walk through the first gate, he was suddenly startled by a tremendous pattering that sounded as if stones were being thrown down onto the drive in front of him. Naturally the man turned and ran, but as soon as he was through the second gate the pattering stopped. Since this event the villagers have been plagued by a phantom clergyman who has appeared a number of times at Wilbury House, accompanied by a small black dog. Whether the two occurrences are linked remains to be seen.

Newton Toney, near Salisbury, Wiltshire

Semley (near Shaftesbury, Dorset)

At Pythouse in Semley a story is told of a scarcely-known girl named Molly, whose ghost is rumoured to haunt the 'Pink Room', where a murder once occurred, as well as the surrounding corridors. A curse warns that if her skull is ever removed from the house then serious misfortune will plague the family responsible. Three times Molly has been removed: the first time a wing of the house caught fire, the second time the son and heir died, and the third time the daughter died.

West Kennet, near Marlborough, Wiltshire

The Long Barrow, or Passing Grave, is the largest of its kind in the country, sitting on a gentle rise not far from Silbury Hill and Avebury. It is a neolithic chamber in which many artefacts were found, suggesting its use by the Beaker people. A local tale tells that on the longest day of the year, at sunrise, a ghostly priest enters the tomb followed by a large hound, which is completely white but for a pair of red ears.

Bridport

Skulls and similar objects have been known to be troublesome additions to a property, perhaps the most famous being the skull that screams if it is ever taken out of Bettiscombe Manor, near Bridport.

BATH

Bladud, Leil's son, a magician, was the ninth King of the Britons and built Bath, calling it Caerbathon; the English later called it Achamannus's city, but finally it was called Bathonia, that is, Bath. William of Malmesbury tells us how in this city hot baths surge and spring up; people suppose that Julius Caesar constructed such baths there, but Ranulph cites Geoffrey of Monmouth who, in his book about the British, says that Bladud built these baths.

CAXTON, The Description of Britain *1480*

Bristol Channel   Somewhere in the Bristol Channel, between Somerset and the Pembroke coast, lie a tiny cluster of fairy islands known locally as the 'Green Meadows of Enchantment'. They are not visible to the human eye and are able to disappear at will, but it seems that those who do not seek them will often stumble across the islands quite by accident.

Bincombe, Dorset   During the sixteenth-century this small village was home to Conjuror Mynterne, a local squire of the manor who dabbled in magic and witchcraft. Legend has it that whilst out riding on Batcombe hill one morning, he suddenly remembered his book of spells which he had left open on his desk. Concerned that someone may read it and perhaps come to harm by interfering with the dark arts, he rushed home and jumped his horse from the top of the hill right across the village. As he flew over the rooftops, his horse caught one of the four pinnacles surrounding the church tower and knocked it clean away. In spite of this the pair made a safe landing on a field known locally as the 'Pitching Plot', but the power of the magic was so strong that grass would never grow there again.

WINCHESTER

In the country surrounding Winchester there is a hollow in the earth, or cavern, out of which a strong wind always blows, so that no one can stand outside it for any length of time. There is also a lake which turns wood into iron if it remains under the water for a year, so that pieces of wood are fashioned into whetstones. Again, on top of a hill there is a grave; everyone who comes and measures it will find it to be exactly his own length and size and, if a pilgrim kneels down by it, he will immediately be completely refreshed, feeling untroubled by weariness.

CAXTON, The Description of Britain *1480*

Fairy Folk

> ### FAIRY
> *In folklore and legend, a diminutive supernatural being of human shape, with magical powers.*
> Brewers Dictionary of Phrase and Fable

The burial mounds or barrows that characterise Bincombe Hill and Bincombe Down provide evidence that the area was extensively settled during the Stone and Bronze Ages. According to local legend, however, these hillocks provide shelter for a community of fairy-folk who have made the area their home. If you are present at Bincombe at midday and put your ear to the ground, you may hear the sound of a fairy orchestra far below your feet.

Bincombe, Dorset

Within the village of Stogursey lies Wick Barrow, a Bronze Age burial mound that is locally associated with pixies. Legend has it that many years ago, a ploughman working close to the mound heard a small child crying in the bushes nearby. The child was complaining that it had broken its peel – a wooden shovel once used for putting loaves into traditional baking ovens – and yet, when the ploughman went to look he found only a small peel with a broken handle. In the hope that the child would eventually come back for the toy, he mended the shovel and hid it in the bushes once more. When he had finished his work for the day, he returned to the spot where he had left the peel to see if it had been taken. It was gone and in its place lay his reward: a freshly baked cake from the pixies' oven.

Stogursey, Somerset

According to British tradition, fairy-folk dwell in an underworld referred to as 'Annwfn'. Portals allow them access into our world and one such portal exists on Glastonbury Tor. Perhaps it is in the series of seven terraces that encircle the Tor. The configuration may be that of a prehistoric maze which also would have had seven circuits. Mazes have always had a magical significance and are often thought of in conjunction with fairies. It is believed that they link our world with another and in this case may act as a portal to 'Annwfn'.

Glastonbury, Somerset

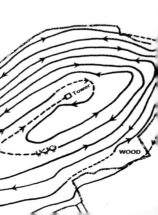

Stourpaine, near Blandford Forum, Dorset

Fairies had a reputation for ringing the bells of Stourpaine Church early in the morning, unless they saw footprints in the dew. The poor unfortunate to whom the offending feet belonged would have bad luck. The message here is plain – fairies do not want to be seen by humans, so the small door and staircase at Stourpaine Church should only be used by ordinary people when the dew has gone; by that time the fairies, too, will have disappeared.

Animal Magic

THE WINTERSLOW LION

On Sunday evening as the Exeter mail coach was proceeding from this city to London, and had stopped as usual at Winterslow Hut . . . the coachman had no sooner pulled up, than the off-leader of his horses was suddenly seized by a lioness (belonging to a menagerie on its way to our fair) which he perceived had just broken loose from a caravan on the side of the road. The lioness sprung upon the horse in the most ferocious manner, seizing him by the throat, and at the same time fasting the talons of her fore paws into the upper part of the horse's neck, and lacerating various parts of his body with the talons of her hind legs. Observing the imminent peril in which his horse was placed, the coachman called aloud for help, and the proprietor and keepers of the menagerie came to the spot, when a large Newfoundland dog belonging to the proprietor instantly seized the lioness by the leg, which occasioned her to quit the horse, and she directly fell upon the dog, and wounded him severely with her teeth and talons (but did not kill him . . .). The guard of the coach was at this time desirus of destroying the lioness by discharging his blunderbuss at her, but was prevented by the proprietor of the animal; and the coach passengers, who were of course much alarmed at the sight of so terrific a creature, escaped into the public house, where they fastened themselves in. The lioness desisted from attacking the dog, on hearing the voices of the keepers, and retired underneath a staddle granary close by where she was shortly afterwards secured, and replaced in the caravan . . .

The lioness is an uncommonly fine young animal, only five years old, and the manner in which she was secured after her attack on the horse affords a remarkable proof of the extreme state of tameness to which such ferocious creatures are brought by the management of their keepers: when she had retired under the staddle granary her owner and assistants, after a short deliberation, followed her upon their hands and knees, with lighted candles, and having placed a sack on the ground near her, they made her lie down upon it: they then tied her four legs, and passed a cord round her mouth, which they secured; in this state they drew her out from under the granary, upon the sack, and then she was lifted andcarried by six men into her den in the caravan.

SALISBURY AND WINCHESTER JOURNAL

Wherwell, Hampshire	The Wherwell Cockatrice was hatched from a duck's egg, in a priory dungeon, by a toad. It grew into a human-eating monster, even devouring nuns from the abbey. After many had been killed trying to win the large rewards on offer for slaying the beast, a man arrived with a large mirror. The cockatrice mistook its reflection for a rival and beat itself to death against the mirror. On Wherwell Church there used to be a weather vane showing the cockatrice. It has since been taken down and was last recorded at Andover museum.
Bryanston School, Dorset	The school was formerly Bryanston House, owned by the Portmans who used to keep peacocks in the grounds. A family legend told that if the peacocks were ever sold off or disappeared, then the family would suffer the same fate. Shortly before his death the third Viscount Portman did sell the birds, and shortly afterwards the family house became the public school of today.
Shapwick, near Wimborne, Dorset	Seaweed used to be strewn on the fields here as fertiliser, and the tale of the Shapwick Monster grew from an incident connected with this practice. A simple, local lad was unloading a freshly arrived cartload of seaweed, when he suddenly dropped his pitchfork in terror at the sight of a crawling sea monster. He ran away to warn his friends who returned with him to witness the creature. None had seen anything like it before. At that moment, however, a man from a different village passed by and, on being shown the monster, could not keep back his laughter. When he had recovered himself he informed them that this was what normal people called a crab. Today the crab is still emblazoned on the caps of the Shapwick cricket team.
Burley, Hampshire	Burley Beacon was once occupied by a large dragon. Every day it flew to the nearby town of Bisterne to demand a pail of milk from the local villagers. The villagers willingly fulfilled the dragon's request and in return he promised to leave their flock of sheep well alone. However, over time the local people tired of the greedy beast and eventually hired a knight to slay him. The knight doused himself with birdlime and ground glass to protect himself against the dragon's fiery breath, and killed him after a fierce and bloody battle. Today there is still a Dragon Lane at Bisterne and a carved dragon can be seen at the entrance to Bisterne Park.

Pigs may not be able to fly but cows appear to think they can. The 150 ft. pillar monument, at a popular picnic area overlooking the Somerset Levels, is known variously as the Parkfield Monument, the Burton Steeple and the Pysent Tower. It was built in 1767 with an inside staircase and access at the top to venture outside and see the panorama. One such adventurer, according to a local story, was a cow that went up three times. Twice she was encouraged down safely, but the third time vertigo seemed to have got the better of her. Cows, alas, like pigs, cannot fly . . . nor, unfortunately, can they land safely.

Burton Pysent, near Somerton, Somerset

Many years ago a huge fiery dragon called Blue Ben lived within Putsham hill. In order to escape the summer heat he would immerse himself in the nearby sea, but his progress was always slowed by the mudflats that stood between his tunnel and the water. One day, as he set about building himself a causeway of rocks into the water, he was discovered by the Devil. Having found Blue Ben's lair, the Devil began to harness him and ride him round the streets of Hell. This upset the dragon as he always found himself getting far too hot. On one occasion, after a particularly exhausting ride, the dragon ran along the causeway in order to reach the cooling water. In his hurry he slipped and fell into the mud where he drowned. A fossilised sea-creature found near Glastonbury in the 1880s may have been Blue Ben.

Burton Pysent, near Somerton, Somerset

BERWICK ST JOHN

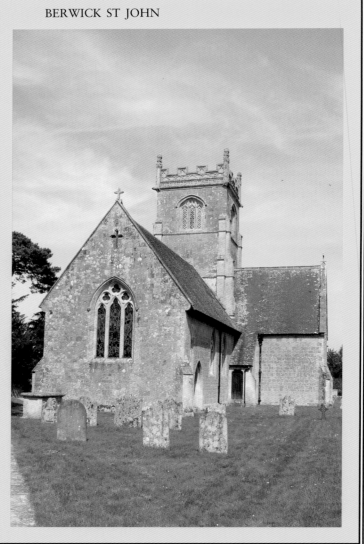

In 1735 the local rector, John Gane, left money to pay for a bell to be rung for fifteen minutes every winter's night as a guide to people travelling on the Downs. This is done from September to March. The village is tucked away in the little valley of the River Ebble, beneath Winkelbury Hill from which there are, perhaps ironically vast and far reaching views on clear days to the Salisbury Cathedral spire, the Isle of Purbeck, the Quantocks, Poole Estuary, Christchurch Priory, the Isle of Wight and the New Forest.

Gussage St Andrew (smallest of the Gussages)

Did Judas hang himself from a tree? According to the twelfth-century wall paintings, showing Christ's passion, this was the case. It is thought to be the only example in the whole of Britain showing such a version of Judas' fate.

SARUM–WILTON TOURNAMENT

In 1194 Richard ordered Hubert, Archbishop of Canterbury, to arrange five tournaments to be held in various places in England, the first to be on a site between Sarum and Wilton . . . The tournament ground was in a wonderful situation on the high ground between the Avon and the Nadder, and opposite to the gates of the castle of Old Sarum. The present Salisbury had not then been built, and the spectators of the tournament could look across the flat marsh from which one day Salisbury Cathedral would rise, to the palace of Clarendon in its lofty position facing the fortress of Old Sarum. To the west could be seen the great buildings of Wilton Abbey with its church, which was in itself almost like a cathedral. The assemblage on the great day fully justified the preparations made beforehand. The villagers from far and near – from Woodford, from Winterbourne, from Wishford, from Fovant, from Newton, from Wylye, from Stapleford, from Britford, from Downton, from Alderbury and from countless other villages – began a day or two before to approach the tournament ground on foot. Early on the morning of the day the main procession issued from the great western portal of the castle itself, the armed men with their banners, their badges and their glittering arms; they were followed by a dingier procession consisting of cowled ecclesiastics, followed by all the numberless hangers-on and retainers of the castle. Meanwhile, from the direction of Wilton, there appeared a very royal procession, for the Abbey was still the place of education for most princesses of the day, and this tournament was a rare treat for the schoolgirls. Close behind them, too, was another procession from St John's Priory at Ditchampton. This was an establishment of the crusading knights of Jerusalem, and its inmates were half-soldiers and half priests. They followed their Prior in great number.

Finally a very gaily dressed procession of courtiers and officials came from the palace of Clarendon, most of them riding on horseback, though some of the ladies were carried in litters. All this preliminary pageantry made the day already worth while for the village people who had walked so far to see it.

EDITH OLIVIER Wiltshire

Winchester,
Hampshire

St Swithin's Day, which falls on 15 July, is relevant, amongst many other things, to King Alfred's major capital. In AD 862, the dying Swithin asked to be buried in the churchyard of the cathedral 'where the drops of rain might wet his grave'. The monks, however, decided to bury him in the choir of the building. A great storm is supposed to have then blown up and poured rain on the mourning procession. The downpour lasted forty days without stopping. Hence the rhyme:

> 'St Swithin's day if thou dost rain
> For forty days will it remain;
> St Swithin's Day if thou art fair,
> For forty days 'twill rain nae mair'.'

Meteorological records do not give any consistency to this claim.

Another piece of folklore attached to that day is that before it apples were not ready for eating: 'Till St Swithin's Day be past / Apples be not fit to taste.' Ralph Whitlock, that great Wiltshire countryman, remembers from early in the 1900s that: 'When I was at school we believed this and refrained from helping outselves to apples until the proper date. From that date on 'fallers' can be used for making tarts or jam . . .'

Cothelstone, near
Taunton,
Somerset

Springs and wells are often regarded as holy and as cures for specific ailments. St Agnes' well, in the Quantock hills, has a very specific traditional cure. St Agnes is the patron saint of young virgins and it is thought that supplicants to this spot were love-sick. On St Agnes's Eve – 21 January – young female virgins would expect to dream of the man they would marry. Before Christianity this well would probably have been a pagan fertility spring.

St Lawrence's Church, a thousand years old and a uniquely Saxon building, is as tall as it is long, and twice as high as it is wide, with reputedly the narrowest chancel arch in England. The saint is said to have discovered the quarries at Hazelbury from which came the stone for the church. When he was out riding near Box, he threw down a glove and told his men that they would find treasure here, which they apparently did.

Bradford on Avon, Wiltshire

At this tiny Bourne Valley hamlet reside the unknown Ladies of Idmiston. They are carved into the stone corbels carrying the roof timbers of this partly twelfth-century church, and are surrounded by men and angels playing music and carrying shields.

Idmiston, near Amesbury, Wiltshire

The Pack Fair at Sherborne has always been a major Wessex fair, held on the first Monday after the feast of St Michael. It was also originally known as Pack Monday Fair. Like all such fairs it was a holiday when all the local people and traders from miles away would assemble for a combination of a market and of revelry. The origin of the name 'Pack' is not entirely clear. St Michael's Day (Michaelmas Day) is the 29th September, or, as still in parts of Cornwall, 10th October. This discrepancy as with all such traditional feasts, including Christmas itself, is caused by the change over to the Gregorian Calendar when 11 days were 'lost'. One explanation for 'Pack' is that pedlars and traders came with their wares and personal belongings wrapped up in bundles or packs. Another relates to the date in 1490 when Abbot Peter Ramsam's workmen completed the nave of the abbey 'packed' up their tools.

Sherborne

**Salisbury,
Wiltshire**

The exact site of the cathedral was determined by Bishop Herbert Poore (1194-1217) who ordered a bowman to fire an arrow from Old Sarum. The new cathedral would be built where the arrow fell. The arrow hit a stag who, mortally wounded, ran to Marysfield where it fell dead. At this place the new cathedral was built.

A well documented and still existing tradition at the cathedral is that of the Boy Bishop. The festival of St Nicholas falls on 6 December and was always well celebrated. From the choristers a Boy Bishop was chosen to hold office for three weeks, until December's feast of the Holy Innocents. If he should die during that period he would be buried with full Bishop's honours. A local tradition says that the miniature representation of a Bishop inside the cathedral is one such boy who died after his ordination.

Dating from AD 980, the originally Saxon church of this picturesque village still has the remains of bright coloured murals in the porch. Naturally any church is concerned for the spiritual and moral well being of its congregation. High up on the outside wall of the south transept, facing towards the porch, is carved the warning:

Breamore, near Fordingbridge, Hampshire

AVOYD FORNICATION
The reason for the message is clear, but why in such an obscure position?

Death and the Devil

Charborough, near Wimborne, Dorset

A fear of death is not unreasonable and preparations and odd requests associated with the final resting place are common. Being buried alive was and still is one of the greatest fears. People would request to be buried with a hammer so that they could break out, or to have pins stuck in them in case they were not really dead.

Squire Holnest of Charborough took no chances, being worried that his relatives would not give him a proper burial. He had a coffin made with a glass lid and he organised his employees as pall bearers. Whenever he felt a hint of death he would go to the coffin, lay down, and have the men carry him round the park. These trial runs allowed him to 'come back from the dead' and harangue the men if they got out of step and swayed or banged him. In the coffin was a hammer, chisel and a bottle of strong liquor.

The coffin was found later to have a hole in the lid and animals would never approach the path taken during those trial runs.

Wimborne Minster, Dorset

Predetermining your death is not an accurate science. Anthony Ettrick's tomb in the south wall of the Trinity Church had to have its pre-made date of 1691 altered to 1703, when he actually died. Furthermore, his vow of wanting to be buried neither in nor out of the church and neither below the ground nor above it, explains the odd position of the tomb, which is kept in good repair by the legacy he left for that purpose.

There may be something in the Dorset air that provokes the strange death request to be buried neither in nor out of a church. Why such a request should be made is unclear, but the tomb is half in and half out of Portesham Church where:

> 'William Weare lies here in dust
> As thou and I and all men must
> Once plundered by Sabean force [the Roundheads]
> Some cald it war but others worse
> With confidence he pleads his cause
> And kings to be above these laws
> September's eyghth day died hee
> When near the date of 63
> Anno Domini 1670'.

Another odd deathbed request was that of the Reverend Edward Bragge of the parish church. He had always loved good food and good wine, so much so that, on being at death's door, his request was to be buried in the dining table that had served his gourmet lifestyle so well. His friends carried out his wish by using the wood from the table to make his coffin.

The tomb of William Longespee Earl of Salisbury (died 7th March 1226), was opened in 1791. Inside Longespee's skull excavators found a dead rat curled up. Amazingly the rat was well preserved with much of its skeleton and fur intact. Rumours persist that the Earl had been poisoned! Was the rat the second victim of an unknown Medieval murderer? Today the rat is on display inside the Salisbury Museum.

Broadway, Somerset

In spite of all the practice he appears to have had, the Devil has never been a very accurate marksman, particularly when hurling large rocks and stones. Broadway Church owes its position to 'Old Nick'. Being cross with Broadway's populace, the Devil threw three large stones at them from Castle Neroch. One landed down Hare Lane, another at Staple Fitzpaine, and the third could not be found. For safety reasons the Broadway inhabitants decided to move the church to where it is now, at the village centre.

Churchstanton, near Wellington, Somerset

The tradition of putting a stake through the heart is not confined to the seekers of vampires. It was also common practice in medieval times when burying a suicide at a crossroads. Suicides had flouted God's law and were not allowed burial in consecrated ground. It was feared their troubled souls would haunt their past places and a crossroads would confuse the ghost. Being in unconsecrated ground, of course, they were unquestionably bound for Hell. An old local story is told of some youngsters out past midnight, who out of joking bravado summoned the Devil. 'Old Nick' appeared and chased them in their terror. One of the youngsters wanted to stop at the crossroads, but the others said it was not a safe place to be, so they ran on and waited. Then they heard a blood curdling yell followed by silence. The Devil had actually come for a suicide buried at the crossroads, unkindly interred without a stake through the heart. The stake would have prevented the souls from going haunting and thwarted collection by the Devil.

Stanton Drew, Somerset

Close by the River Drew stands a group of three stone circles known as 'The Devil's Wedding'. It is believed that many years ago, a local wedding was followed by music and dancing that continued late on into the night. When midnight arrived the piper put down his pipe and made as if to leave for his religion forbade him to play on a Sunday. At that moment an old man appeared and offered to continue in place of the piper. His music was so exhilarating that the dancers could not stop and the faster he played, the faster they danced. All too late the villagers realised that their musician was in fact the Devil himself and before they could stop him the fiend had turned them all to stone.

Great Bedwyn, near Marlborough, Wiltshire

The stonemasons yard of 'Lloyd's' is a treasure trove of unusual, historic tombstones and stonemason's lore, explaining some of the hidden humour of epitaphs and headstone shapes. Even pets are remembered, such as the terrier who left an impression as an actor:

> Very small and very bold
> He always died when he was told.

Potterne, near Devizes, Wiltshire

We do not necessarily know what John Ford did to his wife, but we know that everyone else had an idea and that he is marked forever as his wife's gravestone shows:

> 'Here lies Mary the wife of John Ford
> We hope her soul has gone to the Lord;
> But if for Hell she has changed this Life
> She had better be there than be John Ford's wife.'

The Unexplained

The Bristol Channel to the north and the English Channel to the south can be seen from this 700 foot high ridge, which can perhaps claim to be the most sinister and ominous place in Somerset. The Devil, all manner of ghosts, UFOs, weird shapes, odd shapes and terrible events are associated with it, not to mention the more mundane horrors of highwaymen, smugglers and robbers who used the Windwhistle Inn as a headquarters as this was a major route between London and the West Country.

Of all the myriad tales and events to choose from perhaps the book *Mirabilis Annus* of 1662 gives a flavour of this remote area. A medieval version of UFOs was seen, not by one or two individuals, but by whole groups of people in Chard and Crewkerne, situated at each end of the ridge. Two suns appeared simultaneously in the sky on the evening of 12th July, followed by three moons at around 10 pm on the 14th. On the 19th again two suns were recorded. The next day of the 20th, about an hour after sunset, a long blue cloud drifted from the west over the village of Chillington, on the north side of the ridge. From the cloud a giant appeared, holding a rod in his hand. He then vanished making way for another giant on horseback, wearing a round, flat hat, carrying a sword, and with a long sheath at his side. He disappeared, then an entire battle took place in the sky, between giant figures, with several companies on foot and horse that marched towards each other, one army from the east, one from the west. The soldiers were dressed in armour and carried muskets, whilst the horses were fitted out in full battle colours. They all charged. After a tumultuous and noisy battle the skies quietened and subsided, the armies dissipated. An explanation is still awaited.

Flowers Barrow, Dorset

At the western end of the Purbeck Hill, this Iron Age hill fort has never lost its strategic importance. One army, a Roman garrrison, seems never to have left. Over the centuries the soldiers have been spotted marching the area, intent on reaching some distant rendezvous.

The last recorded sighting was in 1970 when they were spotted at Knowle Hill, near Corfe. Before that they had appeared several times during the Second World War, as well as just prior to it in 1939 and at earlier times of national crisis right back to 1678 when they marched undaunted along the Ridgeway.

Swindon, Wiltshire	This town is the largest and most industrialised in the county, owing to its initial prosperity from the railways which came in the 1840s. A legend explains the site's importance and the building of the Great Western Railway here. Isambard Kingdom Brunel, the great engineer, came on a picnic and threw a sandwich to indicate the spot where the first building should be placed.
Cadnam, New Forest, Hampshire	The Rufus Stone, commemorating the killing whilst out hunting of William Rufus, the 'Red King', is a well known monument in the area. It was erected in 1745 by Earl de la Warr. The arrow which did the killing is supposed to have been shot by Walter Tirel by mistake during the hunt. Others, though, think that Rufus' younger

brother Henry, heir to the throne, organised the shooting, the arrow being fired by the King's Chief Hunter, Ranulf de Aquis. Just outside Ringwood, at Avon Tyrell, is the site of the forge where Tirel is supposed to have made the blacksmith reverse his horse's shoes so that its footprints seemed to be going in the opposite direction.

Piddletrenthide (near Dorchester), Dorset	The dissemination of culture is an odd process. Until the sixteenth century the use of Roman numerals was widespread throughout England. It is strange, then, that a remote village church in Dorset should have an inscription from a hundred years earlier using Arabic numerals when the writing itself is in actual Latin: 'Est pydeltrenth villa in dorsedie comitatu Nascitur in illa quam rexit Vicriatu 1487.' (It is in Piddletrenthide, a town in Dorset [where] he was born [and] where he is Vicar, 1487.) The inscription is over the tower's west door.

The Unexpected

PORTLAND

What an unforgettable experience it is to walk in the mighty bed from which, at the command of Wren, St Paul's arose to stand guard on Ludgate Hill. As I walked along the dusty roads of the island, which dazzle the eyes like snow in sunlight, I thought not only of the buildings which Portland has already given to London, but of the London to be which we will never walk, that slumbers still in darkness in the womb of this pregnant Isle.

H V MORTON, In Search of England

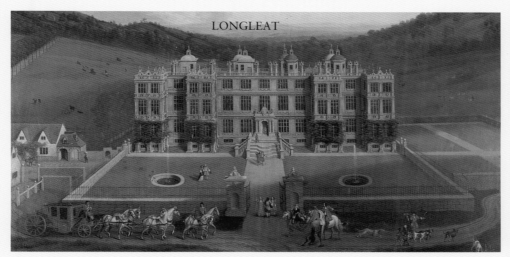

LONGLEAT

The only way to make Bath stone free of another part of the country is the way chosen by Sir John Thynne, in the sixteenth century, when he bought a large area of the Box Quarry and transplanted it bodily to build his palace at Longleat. But even so the stone could only be adapted to fit the architect's plan by putting into the walls almost as much glass as stone, and now no one would dream of calling Longleat a building in the Cotswold manner.

EDITH OLIVIER Wiltshire

Trent (near Yeovil), Somerset	In the church opposite the Manor House is an unusual inscription on a plain white slab:

m

D   A. W.

t

O B   JUL 19

o   m

A   n   D 1698

This is the resting place of Colonel Wyndham's wife Dame Alice. The Wyndhams gave sanctuary to King Charles II. The King arrived on 17th September 1651, fleeing from his defeat at the Battle of Worcester, disguised as the servant of Jane Lane. At the Restoration of the King the Wyndhams were rewarded with a gift of £1,000, a baronetcy, and a pension of £100. The two servants who had waited on the secret guest each received £100.

Bridport, Dorset

A town of 120 houses at the time of Edward the Confessor, Bridport was then one of four Dorset towns that had the right to issue its own coins (Dorchester, Shaftesbury and Wareham being the others). A misconception arose that it was famous for manufacturing daggers. To be 'stabbed with a Bridport dagger' actually meant to be hanged with a rope. The town was well known, being a fishing port, for making good ropes, lines and nets.

Tarrant Rushton (near Wimborne), Dorset

In the east face of the chancel wall we find the medieval answer to today's loudspeakers. Two clay pots were put in the wall to amplify the priest's voice, dating from around 1458, and are the earliest known example in England. Ninety years later Wimborne Minster's records show that their two pots cost 8d and that they were for the 'wyndfylling of the Church'.

Sixpenny Handley, Wiltshire

This unusual name was for a long time misleadingly abbreviated on a signpost near the Dorset–Wiltshire border as '6ᴰ Handley". The name is actually of Saxon origin where the place had two 'hundreds'. One was called Sexpena (meaning 'hill of the Saxons') and the other Hanlega (meaning 'high wood or clearing'). Given local usuage of the names over the centuries the combined name became as it is today.

Nunney (near Frome), Somerset

The ruins of the castle, built by Sir John Delamere in 1373, stand in the very centre of the village, in a position that was not easy to defend. In the Civil War the Cromwellian forces under Fairfax reduced the Royalist castle to its present day condition. He was not fooled by an ingenious defensive strategy tried as a last resort by the Royalist occupants. Each morning the solitary remaining pig had its ears violently tweaked. Naturally this made it squel very loudly and persistently. Fairfax and his men were supposed to conclude from the racket that the castle had plenty of pig meat and was therefore well provisioned to withstand a long siege.

County by County

DORSET

GATCOMBE
It is said that the magical Conjuror Mynterne lived here many years ago.

BINCOMBE
A town inhabited by fairies.

BRYANSTON SCHOOL
Once home to the Portman family whose fate was intrinsically tied to the disappearance of their peacocks.

CERNE ABBAS
Site of the infamous chalk giant.

CHARBOROUGH
The final resting place of Squire Holnest who was buried with a hammer, a chisel and a bottle of strong liquor.

CHARMOUTH
The Reverend Edward Bragge, priest of the parish church, is said to have been buried here in a coffin made from the wood of his dining table.

PORTESHAM
William Weare's coffin lies half in and half out of Portesham parish church after his request to be buried neither on the inside, nor the outside of the building (see also Wimborne).

SHAPWICK
Where a local boy once mistook a crab for a sea monster.

SHERBORNE
The manor house at Sandford Orcas is one of the most haunted buildings in the country.

STOURPAINE
Fairies are said to ring the bells of the church early in the morning.

STURMINSTER
Site of a bridge haunted by the victims of a fatal car accident.

WIMBORNE
Anthony Ettrick's tomb lies half in and half out of the parish church after his strange burial request (see also Portesham).

HAMPSHIRE

AVON TYRELL
Legend tells that this is the site of a forge where Walter Tirel made a blacksmith reverse his horse's shoes. Tirel wanted to appear as if he was moving backwards.

CADNAM
The Rufus stone stands nearby commemorating the killing of William Rufus, the legendary 'Red King'.

EAST WELLOW
Florence Nightingale is said to haunt the parish church.

NEW FOREST
Site of a phantom lake.

WHERWELL
Home to the Wherwell Cockatrice, a flesh-eating monster.

WINCHESTER
The cathedral is thought to be haunted by thirteen phantoms and also provides the setting for the 'Legend of St Swithin'.

SOMERSET

BATH
Setting for the 'Legend of Prince Bladud', a leper who discovered the healing properties of the city's mineral springs.

BURTON PYSENT
Home to a mysterious cow who believed she could fly.

CHURCHSTANTON
The Devil is thought to have visited this town to collect the body of a suicide victim.

COTHELSTONE
St Agnes' well stands in the Quantock hills.

CUDWORTH
The local vicarage is known to be haunted.

GLASTONBURY
Believed to be the site of 'Avalon', a place of great magic and spirituality where King Arthur came to die. Also visited by Joseph of Arimathea, once with his nephew Jesus and a second time with a band of missionaries who came bearing the chalice of the Last Supper (the Holy Grail). Glastonbury Tor may also act as a portal to 'Annwfn'.

HOLFORD
The ghost of a bloody and ragged kennel-man walks the hills of the district.

KILVE
It is said that the dragon, Blue Ben, lived nearby at Putsham hill.

STANTON DREW
Site of the Devil's Wedding stone circle.

STOGURSEY
A village associated with pixies.

TAUNTON
Judge Jeffreys haunts the castle grounds.

WILTSHIRE

AMESBURY
Nearest settlement to Stonehenge and the legendary site of Queen Guinivere's death.

BRADFORD ON AVON
St Lawrence discovered treasure here when he threw his glove onto the ground.

LONGLEY BURREL
The ghostly apparition of Reginald de Cogham is said to roam the hills with his head carried under one arm.

MARLBOROUGH
The college is plagued by a phantom that repeatedly throws itself from a window.

NEWTON TONEY
Home of the haunted Wilbury House.

SALISBURY
Legend tells that the exact site of the cathedral was determined by firing an arrow from the grounds of the old cathedral.

SEMLEY
Pythouse in Semley contains the wailing skull of Molly Bennet-Stanford.

SWINDON
The site of the first Great Western Railway building was apparently determined by a sandwich.

Bibliography

Michael Balfour & Bernd Siering, *Megalithic Mysteries*, Parkgate Books, 1992

Trevor Beer, *Walks in Mysterious Devon*, Sigma Leisure 1997

Janet & Colin Bord, *Mysterious Britain*, Paladin 1974

A G Bradley, *Round About Wiltshire*, Methuen & Co 1907

Enid Byford, *Somerset Curiosities*, Dovecote Press 1987

Caxton, *The Description of Britain*, ed. Marie Collins, Sidgwick & Jackson 1988

John C Chadwick, *Wessex Peculiar – a search for the unusual*, Nigel J Clarke Publications 1986

Dartnell & Goddard, *Wiltshire Words*, Wiltshire Life Society at Avebury Barn 1991

Jane Herbert, *We Wander in Wessex*, Ward, Lock & Co 1947

Garry Hogg, *Odd Aspects of England*, David & Charles 1968

J A Leete, *Wiltshire Miscellany*, Colin Venton Ltd 1976

Rodney Legg, *Mysterious Dorset*, Dorset Publishing Co, 1998

HV Morton, *In Search of England*, Methoen 1927

Edith Olivier, *Wiltshire*, Robert Hale 1951

George Osborn, *Dorset Curiosities*, Dovecote Press 1986

Kingsley Palmer, *Oral Folk Tales of Wessex*, David & Charles 1973

Shane Scott (ed.), *The Hidden Places of Somerset*, Travel Publishing Ltd 1997

Elisabeth Stuart, *Devon Curiosities*, Dovecote Press 1989

Ken Watts, *Exploring Historic Wiltshire 1 & 2*, Ex Libris 1998

Ralph Whitlock, *March Winds & April Showers: Country Weather Lore*, Ex Libris 1993

Ralph Whitlock, *Whitlock's Wessex*, Moonraker Press 1975

Ralph Whitlock, *Wiltshire Folklore & Legends*, Hale 1992

Charles Whynne-Hammond, *Ten Somerset Mysteries*, Countryside Books 1995

Acknowledgements

The publishers gratefully acknowledge the help of Cathy Warren in the preparation of this guide.

Pictures are by courtesy of:

John Crook, p.26

Rob Drake, pp. 3, 6, 10 (top), 14, 17

James Fox, pp. 18, 21, 29

John Fuller, pp. 19, 24

Marquess of Bath, p. 27

Matthew Harvey, Cover panel, pp. 7, 13, 22, 23

Neville Hill, pp. 10 (bottom), 30

Lady Iveagh, p. 5

Andrew Jamieson, Cover border, p. 6

Geoff Roberts Photography, p. 16

Somerset Archaeological and Natural History Society, p. 4

Published by Wessex Books 2004

Text © Roger Crisp

Designed and edited by Jane Drake

Design © Wessex Books 2004

Printed by John Dollin Printing Ltd

ISBN 1-903035-15-5